To:

_____

May the Lord of peace himself give you

peace at all times and in every way.

~2 Thessalonians 3:16

From:

_____

Requests for information should be addressed to:
Inspirio, The gift group of Zondervan
Grand Rapids, Michigan 49530
http://www.inspiriogifts.com

Editor: Janice Jacobson
Design Manager: Amy J. Wenger
Cover/Interior Design: Amy E. Langeler

Printed in China

03 04 05/HK/ 3 2 1

More of
God's Words of Life
for
W·O·M·E·N

inspirio™

~GOD'S WORDS OF LIFE ON~

ACCEPTANCE

*Do to others as you would
have them do to you.*

LUKE 6:31

*Jesus said, "He who receives you receives me,
and he who receives me receives the one who sent me."*

MATTHEW 10:40

*Jesus said, "I have set you an example that
you should do as I have done for you."*

JOHN 13:15

How good and pleasant it is
when brothers live together in unity!

PSALM 133:1

*May the Lord make your love increase
and overflow for each other and for everyone else.*

1 THESSALONIANS 3:12

*Jesus said, "You have heard that it was said,
'Love your neighbor and hate your enemy.'
But I tell you: Love your enemies and pray
for those who persecute you."*

MATTHEW 5:43–44

*To love God with all your heart,
with all your understanding and with
all your strength, and to love your neighbor
as yourself is more important than all
burnt offerings and sacrifices.*

MARK 12:33

*Jesus said, "I tell you the truth, anyone who
gives you a cup of water in my name
because you belong to Christ will
certainly not lose his reward."*

MARK 9:41

*Be devoted to one another in brotherly love.
Honor one another above yourselves.*

ROMANS 12:10

Jesus said, "My command is this: Love each other as I have loved you. Greater love has no one than this, that he lay down his life for his friends."

JOHN 15:12–13

Let us consider how we may spur one another on toward love and good deeds.

HEBREWS 10:24

If you really keep the royal law found in Scripture, "Love your neighbor as yourself," you are doing right.

JAMES 2:8

Dear friends, let us love one another, for love comes from God. Everyone who loves has been born of God and knows God.

1 JOHN 4:7

OVERLOOKING OUR DIFFERENCES

*R*AIN, SLEET OR SNOW, BILL WAS ALWAYS BAREFOOT. WHILE HE was attending college he had become a Christian. At this time a well-dressed, middle-class church across the street from the campus wanted to develop more of a ministry to the students.

One day Bill decided to worship there. He walked into this church, wearing his blue jeans, tee shirt and of course no shoes. People looked a bit uncomfortable, but no one said anything. So Bill began walking down the aisle looking for a seat. The church was quite crowded that Sunday, so as he got down to the front pew and realized that there were no seats, he just squatted on the carpet.

Suddenly an elderly man began walking down the aisle toward the boy. The church became utterly silent; all eyes were focused on him. When the man reached Bill, with some difficulty he lowered himself and sat down next to him on the carpet. He and Bill worshiped together on the floor that Sunday. I was told there was not a dry eye in the congregation.

Grace is always that way. It gives without the receiver realizing how great the gift really is. As this man walked alongside his brother and loved him with all that he had received from Christ's love, so must we.

–Rebecca Manley Pippert

AGING

"Even to your old age and gray hairs
    I am he, I am he who will sustain you.
I have made you and I will carry you;
    I will sustain you and I will rescue you,"
    says the LORD.

ISAIAH 46:4

May the LORD bless you from Zion
    all the days of your life;
may you see the prosperity of Jerusalem,
    and may you live to see your children's children.

PSALM 128:5–6

Is not wisdom found among the aged?
    Does not long life bring understanding?

JOB 12:12

Your children will be many,
    and your descendants like the grass of the earth.

JOB 5:25

Children's children are a crown to the aged,
　　and parents are the pride of their children.

PROVERBS 17:6

Honor your father and your mother,
so that you may live long in the land
the Lord your God is giving you.

EXODUS 20:12

Even when I am old and gray,
　　do not forsake me, O God,
till I declare your power to the next generation,
　　your might to all who are to come.

PSALM 71:18

Teach us to number our days aright,
　　that we may gain a heart of wisdom, O Lord.

PSALM 90:12

Gray hair is a crown of splendor;
  it is attained by a righteous life.

PROVERBS 16:31

[The righteous] will still bear fruit in old age,
  they will stay fresh and green,
proclaiming "The LORD is upright;
  he is my Rock, and there is no wickedness in him."

PSALM 92:14–15

Do not forget my teaching,
  but keep my commands in your heart,
for they will prolong your life many years
  and bring you prosperity.

PROVERBS 3:1–2

Long life to you! Good health to you and
your household! And good health
to all that is yours!

1 SAMUEL 25:6

THE PILGRIM
ROAD

*L*ET'S BE HONEST. OLD AGE ENTAILS SUFFERING. I'M ACUTELY aware of this now as I watch my mother, once so alive and alert and quick, now so quiet and confused and slow. We see the preview of "coming attractions," ourselves in her shoes, and ponder what this interval means in terms of the glory of God in an old woman.

It would be terrifying if it weren't for something that ought to make the Christian's attitude toward aging utterly distinct from the rest. We know it's not for nothing (see Ephesians 1:9-10).

In the meantime, we look at what's happening—limitations of hearing, seeing, moving, digesting, remembering; distortions of countenance, figure and perspective. If that's all we could see, we'd certainly want a face-lift or something.

But we're on a pilgrim road. It's rough and steep, and it winds uphill to the very end. We can lift up our eyes and see the unseen: a celestial city, a light, a welcome and an ineffable face. We shall behold him. We shall be like him. And that makes a difference in how we go about aging.

–Elisabeth Elliot

CHANGE

Every good and perfect gift is from above,
coming down from the Father of the heavenly
lights who does not change like shifting shadows.

JAMES 1:17

"I the LORD do not change,"
says the LORD.

MALACHI 3:6

Jesus Christ is the same yesterday
and today and forever.

HEBREWS 13:8

If anyone is in Christ, he is a new
creation; the old has gone,
the new has come!

2 CORINTHIANS 5:17

Listen, I tell you a mystery: We will not all sleep, but we will all be changed—in a flash, in the twinkling of an eye, at the last trumpet. For the trumpet will sound, the dead will be raised imperishable, and we will be changed.

1 CORINTHIANS 15:51–52

Since then you have been raised with Christ, set your hearts on things above, where Christ is seated at the right hand of God. Set your minds on things above, not on earthly things. For you died, and your life is now hidden with Christ in God.

COLOSSIANS 3:1–3

You were taught, with regard to your former way of life, to put off your old self, which is being corrupted by its deceitful desires; to be made new in the attitude of your minds; and to put on the new self, created to be like God in true righteousness and holiness.

EPHESIANS 4:22–24

"See, I am doing a new thing!
       Now it springs up; do you not perceive it?
I am making a way in the desert
       and streams in the wasteland," says the LORD.

ISAIAH 43:19

We know our old self was crucified with
him so that the body of sin might be
done away with, that we should no
longer be slaves to sin—because anyone
who has died has been freed from sin.

ROMANS 6:6–7

"Behold, I will create
       new heavens and a new earth.
The former things will not be remembered,
       nor will they come to mind.
But be glad and rejoice forever
       in what I will create,
for I will create Jerusalem to be a delight
       and its people a joy," says the LORD.

ISAIAH 65:17-18

TRUST THE
GOD OF CHANGE

*L*IFE FOR MOST OF US IS NOT A STEADY-PACED STROLL THROUGH time, with a beginning, a middle, and an end, like a well-constructed play. It's filled with change. We change schools, careers, homes, relationships, and "images" almost as casually as our great-grandparents changed horses.

Not that all change is by choice. A marriage dissolves. Cherished friendships change in character or another person's choice cuts directly across our own, bringing us where we never wanted to be. A career change, voluntary or involuntary, may disrupt our lives. Financial losses sweep away our props. Even geographic change can be disorienting.

For the believer, then, the question is vital: Is our God the Lord of change? Will he be with us in change, especially when it strains our trust to its limit? Ironically, while we trust him with our eternal fate, we may find it difficult to trust him for next month's car payment, a new relationship, or an unexpected turn in our lives. The assumption that the Almighty is unacquainted with the complex people he has made keeps us hanging onto bits and pieces of our lives, deceived by Satan's ancient lie that God does not want the best for us.

In the kaleidoscopic whirl of our life patterns, it can be enormously reassuring to remind ourselves that God is unchanging: "I the LORD do not change" (Malachi 3:6).

–Gini Andrews

CONTENTMENT

*I have learned to be content whatever
the circumstances. I know what it is to be in need,
and I know what it is to have plenty. I have
learned the secret of being content in any and
every situation, whether well fed or hungry,
whether living in plenty or in want. I can
do everything through him who gives me strength.*

PHILIPPIANS 4:11–12

*Godliness with contentment is great gain.
For we brought nothing into the world,
and we can take nothing out of it.
But if we have food and clothing,
we will be content with that.*

1 TIMOTHY 6:6–8

Better a little with the fear of the LORD
than great wealth with turmoil.

PROVERBS 15:16

Better one handful with tranquillity
      than two handfuls with toil
      and chasing after the wind.

ECCLESIASTES 4:6

Keep your lives free from the love of money and be
      content with what you have, because God has said,
      "Never will I leave you;
      never will I forsake you."
So we say with confidence,
      "The Lord is my helper; I will not be afraid.
      What can man do to me?"

HEBREWS 13:5–6

The boundary lines have fallen for me in pleasant places;
      surely I have a delightful inheritance.

PSALM 16:6

*Each one should retain the place in life that the Lord
assigned to him and to which God has called him.*

1 CORINTHIANS 7:17

Be still before the LORD and wait patiently for him;
    do not fret when men succeed in their ways,
    when they carry out their wicked schemes.
Refrain from anger and turn from wrath;
    do not fret—it leads only to evil.
For evil men will be cut off,
    but those who hope in the Lord will inherit
    the land.

PSALM 37:7–9

A happy heart makes the face cheerful.

PROVERBS 15:13

Better a dry crust with peace and quiet
    than a house full of feasting, with strife.

PROVERBS 17:1

That everyone may eat and drink,
and find satisfaction in all
his toil—this is the gift of God.

ECCLESIASTES 3:13

A SIMPLE LIFE
OF CONTENTMENT

*E*CCLESIASTES HAS BEEN DESCRIBED AS A BOOK ABOUT "RHYTHMS and ruts." The Teacher speaks of cycles of birth and death, youth and aging, poverty and wealth, labor and leisure.

But Ecclesiastes also offers hope for breaking out of the rut. In 4:5 the poem alludes to the delicate balance between work and rest. It says that he who lacks ambition and a work ethic "ruins himself." On the other hand, the problem with "two handfuls" is that it leads to "chasing after the wind" (4:6). The person who is motivated by envy will never have enough.

A happy balance is achieved when one holds "one handful with tranquility" (4:6). If we live with a spirit of contentment and gratitude, we have an empty hand to lift in praise, to extend to a needy neighbor, or to help lift up a friend (4:10).

Less is best when it is accompanied by "quiet." In 1 Thessalonians 4:11–12 Paul describes this lifestyle: "Make it your ambition to lead a quiet life, to mind your own business and to work with your hands, just as we told you, so that your daily life may win the respect of outsiders."

> DEAR LORD, HELP ME TO LEAD A SIMPLE LIFE.
> MAY I NOT SLIP INTO FUTILITY AND THE CHAOS
> OF OVERABUNDANCE. AMEN.

–Reverend Dr. Delores Carpenter

ENCOURAGEMENT

Let the morning bring me word of your unfailing
     love, Lord.
     for I have put my trust in you.
Show me the way I should go,
     for to you I lift up my soul.

PSALM 143:8

The LORD is a refuge for the oppressed,
     a stronghold in times of trouble.

PSALM 9:9

God is our refuge and strength,
     an ever-present help in trouble.
Therefore we will not fear, though the earth give way
     and the mountains fall into the heart of the sea,
though its waters roar and foam
     and the mountains quake with their surging.

PSALM 46:1–3

My soul finds rest in God alone;
    my salvation comes from him.
He alone is my rock and my salvation;
    he is my fortress, I will never be shaken.

PSALM 62:1–2

Jesus said, "In this world you will have trouble. But take heart! I have overcome the world."

JOHN 16:33

My flesh and my heart may fail,
    but God is the strength of my heart
    and my portion forever.

PSALM 73:26

When I said, "My foot is slipping,"
    your love, O LORD, supported me.
When anxiety was great within me,
    your consolation brought joy to my soul.

PSALM 94:18–19

The LORD upholds all those who fall
and lifts up all who are bowed down.

PSALM 145:14

Jesus said, "Come to me, all you who are
weary and burdened, and I will give you rest.
Take my yoke upon you and learn from me, for I am gentle
and humble in heart, and you will find rest for your souls."

MATTHEW 11:28–29

God gives strength to the weary
and increases the power of the weak.
Even youths grow tired and weary,
and young men stumble and fall;
but those who hope in the LORD
will renew their strength.
They will soar on wings like eagles;
they will run and not grow weary,
they will walk and not be faint.

ISAIAH 40:29–31

GETTING RID
OF DISCOURAGEMENT

FTER A DAY OF DEALING WITH A CRANKY BABY OR A HOSTILE teenager or a demanding boss or an unsatisfied husband … I can say—no shout—with Elijah, "I've had enough, Lord!" (1 Kings 19:4).

If I'll just follow the Lord's prescription for discouragement, I should be able to regain control of myself and my emotions:

1. Get enough rest (1 Kings 19:5). Ever notice how a short temper is directly related to a short night's sleep? Sometimes short nights cannot be helped (infants must be fed), but as much as possible get a good night's rest.

2. Eat healthy foods on a regular basis (1 Kings 19:6). Five finger licks of raw cookie dough do not a healthy lunch make. Foods high in protein and low in sugar will give you the strength you need for the strains of your day.

3. Spend some quiet time with yourself and the Lord (1 Kings 19:12). There's just no getting around it. No matter how busy you are, time alone with yourself and with your Lord will provide the stability to catch and handle whatever life throws your way.

4. Now go (1 Kings 19:15). There's much to be done. If you can make rules one through three your high priorities, number four will usually take care of itself.

–Jean E. Syswerda

FAITH

*Faith is being sure of what we hope
for and certain of what we do not see.*

HEBREWS 11:1

*Faith comes from hearing the message,
and the message is heard through the word of Christ.*

ROMANS 10:17

*Let us fix our eyes on Jesus, the author and
perfecter of our faith, who for the joy set
before him endured the cross, scorning its
shame, and sat down at the right hand
of the throne of God.*

HEBREWS 12:2

*Jesus said, "I tell you the truth, if you have
faith as small as a mustard seed, you can say
to this mountain, 'Move from here to there'
and it will move. Nothing will be impossible for you."*

MATTHEW 17:20

I will sing of the LORD's great love forever;
> with my mouth I will make your faithfulness
> known through all generations.
I will declare that your love stands firm forever,
> that you established your faithfulness in
> heaven itself.

PSALM 89:1–2

"Have faith in God," Jesus answered. "I tell you the truth, if anyone says to this mountain, 'Go, throw yourself into the sea,' and does not doubt in his heart but believes that what he says will happen, it will be done for him. Therefore I tell you, whatever you ask for in prayer, believe that you have received it, and it will be yours."

MARK 11:22–24

In the gospel a righteousness from God is revealed, a righteousness that is by faith from first to last, just as it is written: "The righteous will live by faith."

ROMANS 1:17

We live by faith, not by sight.

2 CORINTHIANS 5:7

*Without faith it is impossible to please God, because anyone
who comes to him must believe that he exists and that he
rewards those who earnestly seek him.*

HEBREWS 11:6

*Since we have been justified through faith,
we have peace with God through our Lord Jesus Christ.*

ROMANS 5:1

*Though you have not seen him, you love him; and even
though you do not see him now, you believe in him and
are filled with an inexpressible and glorious joy, for you are
receiving the goal of your faith, the salvation of your souls.*

1 PETER 1:8–9

*It is by grace you have been saved, through faith—
and this not from yourselves, it is the gift of God.*

EPHESIANS 2:8

THE WAY
OF FAITH

*G*OD IS EVER SEEKING TO TEACH US THE WAY OF FAITH, AND IN our training in the faith life there must be room for the trial of faith, the discipline of faith, the patience of faith, the courage of faith; and often many stages are passed before we really realize what is the end of faith, namely, the victory of faith.

Real moral fiber is developed through discipline of faith. You have made your request of God, but the answer does not come. What are you to do?

Keep on believing God's Word; never be moved away from it by what you see or feel, and thus as you stand steady, enlarged power and experience is being developed. Often God delays purposely, and the delay is just as much an answer to your prayer as is the fulfillment when it comes.

Abraham, Moses and Elijah were not great in the beginning, but were made great through the discipline of their faith, and only thus were they fitted for the positions to which God had called them.

When God has spoken of his purpose to do, and yet the days go on and he does not do it, that is truly hard; but it is a discipline of faith that will bring us into a knowledge of God which would otherwise be impossible.

–Mrs. Charles E. Cowman

FORGIVENESS

As far as the east is from the west,
>   so far has God removed our transgressions
>   from us.

PSALM 103:12

"Come now, let us reason together,"
>   says the LORD.
"Though your sins are like scarlet,
>   they shall be as white as snow;
though they are red as crimson,
>   they shall be like wool."

ISAIAH 1:18

"I, even I, am he who blots out
>   your transgressions, for my own sake,
>   and remembers your sins no more," says the LORD.

ISAIAH 43:25

Once you were alienated from God and were enemies in your minds because of your evil behavior. But now he has reconciled you by Christ's physical body through death to present you holy in his sight, without blemish and free from accusation.

COLOSSIANS 1:21–22

"If my people, who are called by my name, will humble themselves and pray and seek my face and turn from their wicked ways, then will I hear from heaven and will forgive their sin and will heal their land," says the Lord.

2 CHRONICLES 7:14

In Christ we have redemption through his blood, the forgiveness of sins, in accordance with the riches of God's grace that he lavished on us with all wisdom and understanding.

EPHESIANS 1:7–8

If we confess our sins, God is faithful and just and will forgive us our sins and purify us from all unrighteousness.

1 JOHN 1:9

Who is a God like you,
> who pardons sin and forgives the transgression
> of the remnant of his inheritance?
You do not stay angry forever
> but delight to show mercy.

MICAH 7:18

Blessed are they
> whose transgressions are forgiven,
> whose sins are covered.
Blessed is the man
> whose sin the Lord will never count against him.

ROMANS 4:7–8

Repent, ... and turn to God, so that your
sins may be wiped out, that times of
refreshing may come from the Lord,
and that he may send the Christ,
who has been appointed for you—even Jesus.

ACTS 3:19–20

SPIRITUAL HOUSECLEANING

*M*UCH THAT WE KEEP STORED IN BOXES IS NOT VALUABLE TO anyone but us. Ticket stubs, blackened corsages, graduation programs are worthless. Yet we keep collecting, preserving memories of important occasions.

There are happy memories and sad ones. Perhaps some bitter ones. We remember angry words and hurt feelings. The relative who didn't come to our wedding. The daughter-in-law who told us to stop interfering. We keep these in our mental storage boxes, getting them out from time to time and reliving the experience.

In Isaiah 43:25 God says to his people, "I, even I, am he who blots out your transgressions, for my own sake, and remembers your sins no more." All those terrible things we have done—God cancels them, wipes them out. He doesn't stuff them away in a drawer just in case he wants to drag them out to jog his memory. He obliterates them. He can't remember them any more. God forgives and forgets. And so should we.

As we get older we can get careless about our spiritual housekeeping. Emotional trash can collect. This is a good day to confess it, make amends, and enjoy life free from ugly clutter.

–Jean Shaw

Jesus said, "Look at the birds of the air; they do not sow or reap or store away in barns, and yet your heavenly Father feeds them. Are you not much more valuable than they?"

MATTHEW 6:26

Jesus said, "I am the good shepherd.
The good shepherd lays down his life for the sheep.

"My sheep listen to my voice;
I know them, and they follow me. I give
them eternal life, and they shall never perish;
no one can snatch them out of my hand.
My Father, who has given them to me,
is greater than all; no one can
snatch them out of my Father's hand."

JOHN 10:11, 27–29

The Lord is faithful, and he will
strengthen and protect you from the evil one.

2 THESSALONIANS 3:3

Praise the LORD, O my soul,
      and forget not all his benefits—
who forgives all your sins
      and heals all your diseases,
who redeems your life from the pit
      and crowns you with love and compassion,
who satisfies your desires with good things
      so that your youth is renewed like the eagle's.

PSALM 103:2–5

Jesus prayed, "I will remain in the world no longer, but [my followers] are still in the world, and I am coming to you. Holy Father, protect them by the power of your name—the name you gave me—so that they may be one as we are one."

JOHN 17:11

Do not withhold your mercy from me, O LORD;
      may your love and your truth always protect me.

PSALM 40:11

He who dwells in the shelter of the Most High
will rest in the shadow of the Almighty.

PSALM 91:1

The LORD will keep you from all harm—
he will watch over your life;
the LORD will watch over your coming and going
both now and forevermore.

PSALM 121:7–8

"Do not fear, for I am with you;
do not be dismayed, for I am your God.
I will strengthen you and help you;
I will uphold you with my righteous
right hand."

ISAIAH 41:10

*Jesus said, "Surely I am with you always,
to the very end of the age."*

MATTHEW 28:20

PROTECTION IN
NEW BEGINNINGS

A SINGLE, LONELY BIRD HOVERED OVER A SUBMERGED WORLD. Below her were the results of the catastrophic flood. There was nothing to be seen but water. The world below her was desolate and seemingly without a future. Nowhere could she find a place to hold on to, to set down her tiny foot. She found no rest.

Yet the dove that fluttered around purposelessly was less lonely than she appeared to be. Noah—his name means "he who will bring rest"—had not forgotten her. He waited for her return. When the bird came, she found an outstretched hand, ready to take her into the safety of the ark. Together they were on their way to a new future. The submerged earth would be habitable again.

We can be compared with this dove. We feel lonely and forsaken. We flutter around in a world that increasingly offers less to hold onto in every way. We see little hope for humanity. Spiritually and emotionally we find no rest.

Yet there is someone who cares about us, who watches closely for each individual: God! Through him we can find rest in spite of the catastrophes that harass the world. He offers us a place to stand, and hope, even in an apparently lost world. He offers a new beginning to those of us who return to him.

–Gien Karssen

GRATITUDE

Praise the LORD.
Give thanks to the LORD, for he is good;
      his love endures forever.

PSALM 106:1

My heart rejoices in the LORD;
      in the LORD my horn is lifted high.

1 SAMUEL 2:1

Enter the LORD's gates with thanksgiving
      and his courts with praise;
      give thanks to him and praise his name.

PSALM 100:4

I will extol the LORD at all times;
      his praise will always be on my lips.

PSALM 34:1

Do not be anxious about anything,
but in everything, by prayer and
petition, with thanksgiving,
present your requests to God.

PHILIPPIANS 4:6

Give thanks in all circumstances,
for this is God's will for you in Christ Jesus.

1 THESSALONIANS 5:18

Everything God created is good, and
nothing is to be rejected if it
is received with thanksgiving.

1 TIMOTHY 4:4

Thanks be to God! He gives us
the victory through our Lord Jesus Christ.

1 CORINTHIANS 15:57

Thanks be to God for his indescribable gift!

2 CORINTHIANS 9:15

Give thanks to the LORD, call on his name;
    make known among the nations what he
    has done.

1 CHRONICLES 16:8

Praise the LORD.
I will extol the LORD with all my heart
    in the council of the upright and in
    the assembly.
Great are the works of the LORD;
    they are pondered by all who delight in them.

PSALM 111:1–2

Sing and make music in your heart to the
Lord, always giving thanks to God the Father for
everything, in the name of our Lord Jesus Christ.

EPHESIANS 5:19–20

In Everything
Give Thanks

*H*OW CAN WE HAVE THANKFUL, CONTENTED HEARTS WHEN THE circumstances in our lives are not what we had planned and when they lie outside our control or our power to change?

Let's look at our alternatives. If we are not thankful, we become bitter and angry with God: he is not providing what we "rightfully" deserve. If we are not content, we become rebellious and complaining: after all, he gives our friends everything they pray for—why does he refuse us?

Underlying these complaints and questions lie two errors in our thinking: that God is not trustworthy and that he does not desire our good. When we compare these conclusions with Scripture, we discover how wrong we are! God's Word instructs us that God is sovereignly in control. He is intimately involved with us; he works out his purposes through the events in our lives so that we may be conformed to the image of his Son. The same God who formed the world in six days knows every hair on our heads.

God's love for his people is not determined by the circumstances in our lives. His love is steadfast. Our marital status, career or finances might fluctuate or totally break apart. In spite of that, however, we can and must give him thanks for his love toward us.

-Carol L. Baldwin

GUIDANCE

"I will instruct you and teach you in the way you
should go;
I will counsel you and watch over you," says
the LORD.

PSALM 32:8

*Whether you turn to the right or to the left, your ears will hear
a voice behind you, saying, "This is the way; walk in it."*

ISAIAH 30:21

This God is our God for ever and ever;
he will be our guide even to the end.

PSALM 48:14

Your word is a lamp to my feet
and a light for my path, O LORD.

PSALM 119:105

"I know the plans I have for you,"
declares the LORD, "plans to prosper
you and not to harm you, plans
to give you hope and a future."

JEREMIAH 29:11

The LORD restores my soul.
> He guides me in paths of righteousness
> for his name's sake.

PSALM 23:3

Trust in the LORD with all your heart
> and lean not on your own understanding;
in all your ways acknowledge him,
> and he will make your paths straight.

PROVERBS 3:5–6

Jesus said, "When he, the Spirit of truth,
comes, he will guide you into all truth."

JOHN 16:13

The LORD will guide you always;
>   he will satisfy your needs in a sun-scorched land
>   and will strengthen your frame.
You will be like a well-watered garden,
>   like a spring whose waters never fail.

ISAIAH 58:11

I am always with you; O LORD,
>   you hold me by my right hand.
You guide me with your counsel,
>   and afterward you will take me into glory.

PSALM 73:23–24

*In your unfailing love you will lead the
people you have redeemed. In your strength you
will guide them to your holy dwelling.*

EXODUS 15:13

The LORD will teach us his ways,
>   so that we may walk in his paths.

ISAIAH 2:3

GUIDANCE OR
A GUIDE?

*S*OMETIMES WHEN WE ASK GOD OUR "*WHY*" QUESTIONS, instead of giving us answers he gives us himself—the Comforter. From Luke 11:13 we learn: Even as fathers give good gifts to their children, so our Father gives the best gift, the Holy Spirit, the Comforter, to us as we ask.

It reminded me of conversations with my daughter Jessie about why I wouldn't allow her to sleep over at a friend's house: "I can give you my reasons, but you won't like them or understand them, and you'd only argue with me. So let's just accept that this is the way it's going to be, and I'm sorry you feel sad."

Often when we ask God for guidance, what we really want is a guide. My friend told me of a conversation he had with his young son shortly after they moved into their new house. "You can find your way to your new bedroom in the dark by simply turning on the lights in each room as you go." There was an uncertain pause, then, "But, Daddy, won't you please go with me?"

~Mary Jane Worden

HOLINESS

*Offer your bodies as living sacrifices,
holy and pleasing to God—this is your spiritual
act of worship. Do not conform any longer to the
pattern of this world, but be transformed by the
renewing of your mind. Then you will be able
to test and approve what God's will is—
his good, pleasing and perfect will.*

ROMANS 12:1–2

*Now that you have been set free from sin
and have become slaves to God, the benefit
you reap leads to holiness, and the
result is eternal life.*

ROMANS 6:22

*God chose us in him before the creation
of the world to be holy and blameless in his sight.*

EPHESIANS 1:4

You were taught, with regard to your former way of life, to put off your old self, ... to be made new in the attitude of your minds; and to put on the new self, created to be like God in true righteousness and holiness.

EPHESIANS 4:22–24

Serve God with wholehearted devotion and with a willing mind, for the LORD searches every heart and understands every motive behind the thoughts. If you seek him, he will be found by you.

1 CHRONICLES 28:9

What does the LORD your God ask of you but to fear the LORD your God, to walk in all his ways, to love him, to serve the LORD your God with all your heart and with all your soul.

DEUTERONOMY 10:12

Whatever is true, whatever is noble, whatever is right, whatever is pure, whatever is lovely, whatever is admirable—if anything is excellent or praiseworthy—think about such things.

PHILIPPIANS 4:8

This is what the high and lofty One says—
      he who lives forever, whose name is holy:
"I live in a high and holy place,
      but also with him who is contrite and lowly
      in spirit,
to revive the spirit of the lowly
      and to revive the heart of the contrite."

ISAIAH 57:15

His divine power has given us everything we
need for life and godliness through our
knowledge of him who called us by
his own glory and goodness.

2 PETER 1:3

You are a people holy to the LORD your God.
The LORD your God has chosen you out
of all the peoples on the face of the earth
to be his people, his treasured possession.

DEUTERONOMY 7:6

CREATE IN ME, LORD ... A PURE HEART, YES. BUT FATHER, EVEN more. Create in me ... (out of nothing—for that's what creation means) an expectant heart. I stand on tiptoe waiting each moment in joyous anticipation for what you are going to do! Create in me an enthusiastic heart—en theo—meaning "in God," God in me, filled to overflowing with you, Lord! Create in me a laughing heart— one that sees the serendipities of an autumn leaf and mist upon the mountains and hears the chuckle of a child. Create in me a heart of integrity—to be real, not to talk above my walk, not to try to impress. Create in me a caring heart—tender toward the hurts and happenings of others, more concerned with their needs than with my own. Create in me an attentive heart—able to hear your whisper, and moment by moment listen to your voice. Create in me a contented heart—at peace with the circumstances of life. Create in me a hungry heart—longing to love you more, desiring your Word, reaching ... stretching ... for more of you. Creator Lord, create in me. Amen.

—Carole Mayhall

HOPE

You have been my hope, O Sovereign LORD,
my confidence since my youth.

PSALM 71:5

*We also rejoice in our sufferings, because we know
that suffering produces perseverance; perseverance,
character; and character, hope. And hope does
not disappoint us, because God has poured out
his love into our hearts by the Holy Spirit,
whom he has given us.*

ROMANS 5:3–5

As for me, I will always have hope;
I will praise you more and more, O God.

PSALM 71:14

*Everything that was written in the past was written
to teach us, so that through endurance and the
encouragement of the Scriptures we might have hope.*

ROMANS 15:4

May your unfailing love rest upon us, O LORD,
    even as we put our hope in you.

PSALM 33:22

Put your hope in the LORD,
    for with the LORD is unfailing love
    and with him is full redemption.

PSALM 130:7

Blessed is he whose help is the God of Jacob,
    whose hope is in the LORD his God.

PSALM 146:5

This I call to mind
    and therefore I have hope:
Because of the LORD's great love we are not consumed,
    for his compassions never fail … .
The LORD is good to those whose hope is in him,
    to the one who seeks him.

LAMENTATIONS 3:21–22, 25

May the God of hope fill you with all joy and peace
as you trust in him, so that you may overflow
with hope by the power of the Holy Spirit.

ROMANS 15:13

Since we have been justified through faith,
we have peace with God through our
Lord Jesus Christ, through whom we
have gained access by faith into this grace
in which we now stand. And we rejoice
in the hope of the glory of God.

ROMANS 5:1–2

Why are you downcast, O my soul?
　　　Why so disturbed within me?
Put your hope in God,
　　　for I will yet praise him,
　　　my Savior and my God.

PSALM 42:11

BE JOYFUL IN HOPE

I WONDERED WHY GOD ASKS US TO BE JOYFUL IN HOPE. I CAN understand why he reminds us to be faithful in prayer—so many times in hardships we slack off in prayer. I can also understand why God asks us to be patient in affliction—patience is hard to muster when you're hurting.

But why does God say to be joyful in hope? Obviously, there must be many times when we lack joy in hope. Think about it. The focus of our hope is yet to be fulfilled; we don't yet possess that for which we hope. And you'll agree that it's hard to be joyful about something we don't yet have!

Lying in bed, it hit home that God wants me to be joyful about future things. Just as we have the command to be faithful in prayer and patient in affliction, we have a command to be joyful in hope. How can God command joy? It's easy once we realize what's over the heavenly horizon.

Does the idea of heavenly glories above put a smile on your face? Do you get a charge when you talk about the return of the Lord? Heaven will seem more near and real to you as you stir up your joy over that for which you hope. And remember, it's a command for your own good.

~Joni Eareckson Tada

HOSPITALITY

Jesus said, "I was hungry and you gave me something to eat, I was thirsty and you gave me something to drink, I was a stranger and you invited me in, I needed clothes and you clothed me, I was sick and you looked after me, I was in prison and you came to visit me." Then the righteous will answer him, "Lord, when did we see you hungry and feed you, or thirsty and give you something to drink? When did we see you a stranger and invite you in, or needing clothes and clothe you? When did we see you sick or in prison and go to visit you?" The King will reply, "I tell you the truth, whatever you did for one of the least of these brothers of mine, you did for me."

MATTHEW 25:35–40

Be hospitable, one who loves what is good, who is self-controlled, upright, holy and disciplined.

TITUS 1:8

Do not forget to entertain strangers, for by so doing some people have entertained angels without knowing it.

HEBREWS 13:2

When you give a luncheon or dinner, do not invite your friends, your brothers or relatives, or your rich neighbors; if you do, they may invite you back and so you will be repaid. But when you give a banquet, invite the poor, the crippled, the lame, the blind, and you will be blessed. Although they cannot repay you, you will be repaid at the resurrection of the righteous.

LUKE 14:12–14

Offer hospitality to one another without grumbling. Each one should use whatever gift he has received to serve others, faithfully administering God's grace in its various forms. …If anyone serves, he should do it with the strength God provides, so that in all things God may be praised through Jesus Christ.

1 PETER 4:9–11

Share with God's people who are in need. Practice hospitality.

ROMANS 12:13

*Do not forget to do good and to share
with others, for with such
sacrifices God is pleased.*

HEBREWS 13:16

*This service that you perform is not only
supplying the needs of God's people but is also
overflowing in many expressions of thanks to God.
Because of the service by which you have proved
yourselves, men will praise God for the obedience
that accompanies your confession of the gospel
of Christ, and for your generosity in sharing
with them and with everyone else.*

2 CORINTHIANS 9:12–13

*Jesus said, "Give, and it will be given to you.
A good measure, pressed down, shaken together
and running over, will be poured into your lap.
For with the measure you use, it will
be measured to you."*

LUKE 6:38

HOSPITALITY NEEDED, NOT WEALTH

*S*OME OF US FEEL THAT IT IS A LACK OF MONEY THAT HOLDS US down. Gideon replied to God's request, "But Lord ... how can I save Israel? My clan is the weakest in Manasseh, and I am the least of my family" (Judges 6:15). With no finances behind him at all, Gideon was turned into a wise prophet by God's commanding power.

Many times I have had sweet Christians tell me they cannot have friends in for fellowship because they do not have good china or matching napkins, because their house is too small, or because their talent is too slight. But these are only excuses for our unwillingness to do as God has asked us. "Offer hospitality to one another without grumbling" (1 Peter 4:9). I would enjoy a peanut butter sandwich if someone else prepared it and handed it to me.

The world tells us that we need money to be happy, but as God told Gideon, "I will be with you" (Judges 6:16). Should not his presence be assurance enough?

–Florence Littauer

GOD'S WORDS OF LIFE ON

J O Y

Light is shed upon the righteous
and joy on the upright in heart.

PSALM 97:11

God will yet fill your mouth with laughter
and your lips with shouts of joy.

JOB 8:21

The LORD's favor lasts a lifetime;
weeping may remain for a night,
but rejoicing comes in the morning.

PSALM 30:5

May all who seek you
rejoice and be glad in you;
may those who love your salvation always say,
"Let God be exalted!"

PSALM 70:4

The ransomed of the LORD will return.
      They will enter Zion with singing;
        everlasting joy will crown their heads.
Gladness and joy will overtake them,
      and sorrow and sighing will flee away.

ISAIAH 51:11

Let all who take refuge in you be glad, LORD;
      let them ever sing for joy.
Spread your protection over them,
      that those who love your name may rejoice in you.

PSALM 5:11

Shout for joy to the LORD, all the earth.
      Worship the LORD with gladness;
      come before him with joyful songs.

PSALM 100:1–2

Your statutes are my heritage forever, LORD;
      they are the joy of my heart.

PSALM 119:111

The prospect of the righteous is joy.

PROVERBS 10:28

You will go out in joy
        and be led forth in peace;
the mountains and hills
        will burst into song before you,
and all the trees of the field
        will clap their hands.

ISAIAH 55:12

You have made known to me the paths of life;
        you will fill me with joy in your presence.

ACTS 2:28

Jesus said, "Now is your time of grief,
but I will see you again and you will rejoice,
and no one will take away your joy."

JOHN 16:22

THE SOURCE
OF JOY

WE FIND THAT OUR JOY IS GREATLY AFFECTED BY CIRCUMSTANCES. When everything goes smoothly, we radiate a joyful spirit. But what happens when everything goes wrong, when our world seems to fall apart around us? Our joy seems to "fly out the window."

The source of true joy is the Lord himself. There is a difference between the joy that comes from peaceful circumstances and the joy of the Lord that is constant and enduring day after day regardless of the circumstances about us.

In God's Word we read of the nine Christian virtues which are the fruit of the Spirit: "But the fruit of the Spirit is love, joy, peace, patience, kindness, goodness, faithfulness, gentleness and self-control" (Galatians 5:22–23). We might illustrate this in the following way. A flower has a number of petals, and each petal is an essential part of the complete flower. Joy is one of the "petals" in the fruit of the Spirit, and without it we are not complete Christians.

The joy of the Lord transforms us and gives a cheerfulness and joyousness that is not dependent upon our outward circumstances but comes from the presence of Christ in our hearts. It has been aptly said, "Joy is the flag which is flown from the castle of the heart when the King is in residence there."

-Millie Stamm

KINDNESS

*Carry each other's burdens, and in this
way you will fulfill the law of Christ.*

GALATIANS 6:2

*This is what the LORD Almighty says: "Administer
true justice; show mercy and compassion to one another."*

ZECHARIAH 7:9–10

*Give to the one who asks you, and do not turn away from the
one who wants to borrow from you.*

MATTHEW 5:42

*As we have opportunity, let us do good to all people, especially
to those who belong to the family of believers.*

GALATIANS 6:10

Be kind and compassionate to one another.

EPHESIANS 4:32

As God's chosen people, holy and dearly loved, clothe yourselves with compassion, kindness, humility, gentleness and patience.

COLOSSIANS 3:12

Jesus said, "In everything, do to others what you would have them do to you."

MATTHEW 7:12

Jesus said, "If anyone gives even a cup of cold water to one of these little ones because he is my disciple, I tell you the truth, he will certainly not lose his reward."

MATTHEW 10:42

When the kindness and love of God our Savior appeared, he saved us, not because of righteous things we had done, but because of his mercy.

TITUS 3:4–5

"With everlasting kindness
I will have compassion on you,"
says the LORD your Redeemer.

ISAIAH 54:8

The LORD is compassionate and gracious,
slow to anger, abounding in love.
He will not always accuse,
nor will he harbor his anger forever.

PSALM 103:8–9

An anxious heart weighs a man down,
but a kind word cheers him up.

PROVERBS 12:25

*"Let him who boasts boast about this:
that he understands and knows me,
that I am the LORD, who exercises kindness,
justice and righteousness on earth,
for in these I delight," declares the LORD.*

JEREMIAH 9:24

MEDICINE
CHEST KINDNESS

*Y*ESTERDAY THE DOORBELL RANG, AND A TERRIFIED YOUNG FELLOW hopping up and down on my doorstep tried to tell me that his pal was bleeding to death on the road—massive hemorrhage.

I ran to the site of the accident, where the victim was just untangling himself from the wreckage of his bicycle. Judging from his groans, I thought he had amputated his leg.

Somehow I managed to get him into my bathroom and wash off his wounds. An accurate diagnosis confirmed my suspicions: he had simply scraped the scab from a previous injury. I solemnly conjured up an impressive-looking bandage, and he was back on the road in no time at all, completely cured.

Whether it is a tiny sliver in a chubby finger, or cancer clawing at a ravaged frame, pain demands priority. Why then am I so hesitant in dispensing consolation? Do I wait until an emergency demands it before investing in a "first-aid" kit? Must I first suffer physically, mentally, emotionally, or spiritually before I learn the healing value of a soothing hand, a mutual tear, a sympathizing heart, an understanding word?

Surely I do well to keep my medicine chest well stocked with love and compassion as well as with bandages, for I never know when I will be called upon to deal with tragedy, or when tragedy may call to deal with me.

-Alma Barkman

LISTENING

This is the confidence we have in approaching God:
that if we ask anything according to his will,
he hears us. And if we know that he hears us—
whatever we ask—we know that we
have what we asked of him.

1 JOHN 5:14–15

"Listen, listen to me, and eat what is good,
        and your soul will delight in the richest of fare.
Give ear and come to me;
        hear me, that your soul may live," says the LORD.

ISAIAH 55:2–3

Whoever listens to [wisdom] will live in safety
        and be at ease, without fear of harm.

PROVERBS 1:33

Blessed rather are those who hear
the word of God and obey it.

LUKE 11:28

Pay attention to my wisdom,
      listen well to my words of insight,
that you may maintain discretion
      and your lips may preserve knowledge.

PROVERBS 5:1–2

As the Holy Spirit says:
      "Today, if you hear his voice,
      do not harden your hearts."

HEBREWS 3:7–8

*Jesus said, "Everyone who listens to the
Father and learns from him comes to me."*

JOHN 6:45

*In the past God spoke to our forefathers through the
prophets at many times and in various ways, but in these last
days he has spoken to us by his Son, whom he appointed heir of
all things, and through whom he made the universe.*

HEBREWS 1:1–2

Jesus said, "Here I am! I stand at the door and knock. If anyone hears my voice and opens the door, I will come in and eat with him, and he with me."

REVELATION 3:20

Jesus said, "I tell you the truth. ... The man who enters by the gate is the shepherd of his sheep. The watchman opens the gate for him, and the sheep listen to his voice. He calls his own sheep by name and leads them out. When he has brought out all his own, he goes on ahead of them, and his sheep follow him because they know his voice."

JOHN 10:1–4

He who listens to a life-giving rebuke
will be at home among the wise.

PROVERBS 15:31

You hear, O LORD, the desire of the afflicted;
you encourage them, and you listen to
their cry.

PSALM 10:17

STOP TALKING
AND LISTEN

*I*T HAPPENS ALL THE TIME. YOU GET TOGETHER WITH A FRIEND, or someone you haven't seen in a while, and before you know it, you've filled the air with a lot of talk about … you. You realize in embarrassment that you're rambling on about yourself and have nearly forgotten to include your friend or even God in the conversation. Oh, to be able to use words with restraint.

That's why I love traveling with my husband or my best friends. We are able to relax and be silent in each other's presence. No forced conversations. No filling the air with empty words. What a blessing it is to be able to sit with someone you love, smile at each other occasionally, and enjoy the quiet together. Friendships, whether with others or with God, are deepened in silence.

When you stop talking long enough to listen, you learn something—only in silence can what you hear filter from your head into your heart. Only in silence can you hear the heartbeat of God and His still, small voice. In quiet, you realize spiritual insights that reach far beyond words.

If you meet with a friend today, make a concerted effort to talk less and listen more. It may do wonders for your friendship. And this evening when you retire, say less in your prayer time and devote more moments simply listening to God.

~Joni Eareckson Tada

LOVE

Serve one another in love. The entire law is summed up in a single command: "Love your neighbor as yourself."

GALATIANS 5:13–14

Love is patient, love is kind. It does not envy, it does not boast, it is not proud. It is not rude, it is not self-seeking, it is not easily angered, it keeps no record of wrongs. Love does not delight in evil but rejoices with the truth. It always protects, always trusts, always hopes, always perseveres. Love never fails.

1 CORINTHIANS 13:4–8

May the Lord make your love increase and overflow for each other and for everyone else.

1 THESSALONIANS 3:12

Live a life of love, just as Christ loved us and gave himself up for us as a fragrant offering and sacrifice to God.

EPHESIANS 5:2

*God so loved the world that he gave
his one and only Son, that whoever
believes in him shall not perish
but have eternal life.*

JOHN 3:16

*This is how we know what love is: Jesus
Christ laid down his life for us.*

1 JOHN 3:16

*Above all, love each other deeply,
because love covers over a multitude of sins.*

1 PETER 4:8

*Let us love one another, for love comes from God.
Everyone who loves has been born of God
and knows God. Whoever does not love
does not know God, because God is love.*

1 JOHN 4:7–8

No one has ever seen God; but if we love one another,
God lives in us and his love is made complete in us.

1 JOHN 4:12

The LORD your God is with you,
　　he is mighty to save.
He will take great delight in you,
　　he will quiet you with his love,
　　he will rejoice over you with singing.

ZEPHANIAH 3:17

We love because he first loved us.

1 JOHN 4:19

Jesus said, "A new command I give you:
Love one another. As I have loved you,
so you must love one another. By this all
men will know that you are my
disciples, if you love one another."

JOHN 13:34–35

LOVE
LANGUAGES

*M*Y HUSBAND'S LANGUAGE OF LOVE DOESN'T INCLUDE ROMANTIC walks under the moonlight, holding hands. Ken doesn't go for mushy sentiment. Watching a basketball game together is his idea of romance. But I'm not complaining. I've learned to appreciate his language of love.

I've also learned the Lord's language of love. When I tell Jesus that I love him, it has nothing to do with romance. But passion? Yes! My love for Jesus is not a syrupy sentiment, but it is definitely zealous and fervent, spirited and intense. When I praise him, I believe he deserves adoration filled with warmth and affection. When I sing to him, I want the melody to come right from my heart.

This is the language of love between God and his creation. We should love him this way because this is how he loves us. To love to the point of death is passion with a capital "P." This is the way we are to love our brothers and sisters, too.

Developing an artful language of love to the Lord will cost you something. It will cost you your pride and, most valued of all, your human logic. Throw your caution to the wind and invite the Spirit of God to fill your heart with the warmth and passion of praise.

–Joni Eareckson Tada

PATIENCE

*You need to persevere so that when you have done the will of
God, you will receive what he has promised.*

HEBREWS 10:36

*Everyone should be quick to listen, slow to speak
and slow to become angry.*

JAMES 1:19

Wait for the LORD;
      be strong and take heart
      and wait for the LORD.

PSALM 27:14

*Be joyful in hope, patient in
affliction, faithful in prayer.*

ROMANS 12:12

*Be completely humble and gentle; be patient,
bearing with one another in love.*

EPHESIANS 4:2

*The testing of your faith develops perseverance.
Perseverance must finish its work so that you
may be mature and complete, not lacking anything.*

JAMES 1:3–4

*If we hope for what we do not
yet have, we wait for it patiently.*

ROMANS 8:25

*Keep yourselves in God's love as you
wait for the mercy of our Lord
Jesus Christ to bring you to eternal life.*

JUDE 1:21

*Be patient, ... until the Lord's coming.
See how the farmer waits for the land to
yield its valuable crop and how patient
he is for the autumn and spring rains.
You too, be patient and stand firm,
because the Lord's coming is near.*

JAMES 5:7–8

Let us not become weary in doing good, for at the proper time we will reap a harvest if we do not give up.

GALATIANS 6:9

We pray ... that you may live a life worthy of the Lord and may please him in every way: bearing fruit in every good work, growing in the knowledge of God, being strengthened with all power according to his glorious might so that you may have great endurance and patience.

COLOSSIANS 1:10–11

The end of a matter is better than its beginning,
and patience is better than pride.

ECCLESIASTES 7:8

*The Lord is not slow in keeping his promise,
as some understand slowness. He is patient
with you, not wanting anyone to perish,
but everyone to come to repentance.*

2 PETER 3:9

THE PATIENCE
OF JOB

Y ou've heard of the patience of Job? To me that never made sense, because the book of Job is one long list of complaints. Job cried out in protest against God. Even his friends were shocked at his impudent anger. Most of us would bite our nails in fearful trembling if we ever talked to God that way.

God, however, does not get offended. He doesn't get insulted or intimidated. In fact, in a supreme touch of irony, God orders Job's pious comforters to seek repentance from Job, the very source of so many heated complaints.

I love that about God. Where it concerned Job, the guy was only human. And, yes, his patience was gloriously played out in that he refused to curse God and die. But it was the Lord who demonstrated the very best of what it means to be patient. God, as it says elsewhere in Scripture, refused to break the bruised reed or snuff out the smoldering wick.

The patience of Job? I would think it should be the patience of God. The God of Job—your God—defends the hurting, uplifts the oppressed, and listens to the complaints of the suffering. He may not respond to your questions with neat, pat answers, but he will always, always answer your questions with his own patience.

~Joni Eareckson Tada

PEACE

*Jesus said, "Peace I leave with you; my peace I give you.
I do not give to you as the world gives. Do not let your
hearts be troubled and do not be afraid."*

JOHN 14:27

LORD, you establish peace for us;
     all that we have accomplished you have done
     for us.

ISAIAH 26:12

*Let the peace of Christ rule in your hearts, since as
members of one body you were called to peace.*

COLOSSIANS 3:15

*Do not be anxious about anything, but in
everything, by prayer and petition, with
thanksgiving, present your requests to God. And the peace
of God, which transcends all understanding, will guard
your hearts and your minds in Christ Jesus.*

PHILIPPIANS 4:6–7

I will lie down and sleep in peace,
for you alone, O LORD,
make me dwell in safety.

PSALM 4:8

The LORD gives strength to his people;
the LORD blesses his people with peace.

PSALM 29:11

Blessed are the peacemakers,
for they will be called sons of God.

MATTHEW 5:9

*May the Lord of peace himself give
you peace at all times and in every way.*

2 THESSALONIANS 3:16

You will keep in perfect peace, O LORD,
    him whose mind is steadfast,
    because he trusts in you.

ISAIAH 26:3

The fruit of righteousness will be peace;
    the effect of righteousness will be quietness
    and confidence forever.

ISAIAH 32:17

Great peace have they who love your law,
    and nothing can make them stumble.

PSALM 119:165

*For Jesus himself is our peace, who has
made the two one and has destroyed
the barrier, the dividing wall of hostility.*

EPHESIANS 2:14

BLESSED ARE
THE PEACEMAKERS

*L*AST NIGHT JOE REMINDED ME THAT IT WAS TIME TO START getting the income tax stuff together. I groaned, leaning back against the couch. "How I dread this time of year! Trying to find all the papers."

He raised an eyebrow and I knew what he was thinking. "You don't believe I have a system, do you?

"Hey! Did I say anything? All you have to do is dig out the records."

"But you just watch, some important paper will be missing. Like last year."

His eyebrow went up again. "You must have thrown it out. Like that gift certificate to the Velvet Turtle."

"The Velvet Turtle! You always bring that up." I could tell him about a few other things he'd misplaced—like the whole garage. I started toward the kitchen, and unexpectedly, through Scripture, the Holy Spirit whispered: Blessed are the peacemakers.

I struggled with the Spirit a moment or two before I calmed down. I poured coffee and brought him a cup. "Honey, let's not argue. Things certainly do have a way of disappearing around here." I sat on his chair arm and hugged him. "Only the Lord knows what important things I've thrown out this year."

Alone in the bathroom, I thanked the Lord for closing my mouth before I said anything else. I always bluster the loudest when I feel guilty.

~Mab Graff Hoover & ~Kathryn Hillen

PRAYER

The LORD is near to all who call on him,
to all who call on him in truth.

PSALM 145:18

"Call to me and I will answer you and tell you great and
unsearchable things you do not know," says the LORD.

JEREMIAH 33:3

Jesus said, "I tell you the truth, my Father
will give you whatever you ask in my name.
Until now you have not asked for anything in
my name. Ask and you will receive,
and your joy will be complete."

JOHN 16:23–24

The LORD ... hears the prayer
of the righteous.

PROVERBS 15:29

Delight yourself in the LORD
and he will give you the desires of your heart.

PSALM 37:4

*Jesus said, "When you pray, go into your room,
close the door and pray to your Father, who
is unseen. Then your Father, who sees
what is done in secret, will reward you."*

MATTHEW 6:6

*Is any one of you in trouble? He should pray. Is anyone happy?
Let him sing songs of praise. Is any one of you sick? He should
call the elders of the church to pray over him and anoint him
with oil in the name of the Lord. And the prayer offered in
faith will make the sick person well; the Lord will raise him up.
If he has sinned, he will be forgiven. Therefore confess your sins
to each other and pray for each other so that you may be healed.*

JAMES 5:13–16

This is the confidence we have in approaching God: that if we ask anything according to his will, he hears us. And if we know that he hears us—whatever we ask—we know that we have what we asked of him.

1 JOHN 5:14–15

The eyes of the Lord are on the righteous
and his ears are attentive to their prayer.

1 PETER 3:12

Dear friends, build yourselves up in your most holy faith and pray in the Holy Spirit. Keep yourselves in God's love as you wait for the mercy of our Lord Jesus Christ to bring you to eternal life.

JUDE 1:20–21

"Before they call I will answer;
while they are still speaking I will hear,"
says the LORD.

ISAIAH 65:24

PRAY WITHOUT CEASING

*G*OD EMPHASIZES THE IMPORTANCE OF PRAYER. NEEDS ARE SUPPLIED, problems solved, the impossible accomplished through prayer. Therefore we *ought* to pray. We may not feel like it, but we ought to pray. We may be discouraged, but we ought to pray.

We are *always* to pray—not merely when we have a need or only at some set time, but always. The line to heaven is always open. We are sometimes prone to make our own plans or decisions before we pray, but we should pray about everything first.

Not only are we to pray, but we are not to faint. Perhaps we have been praying about something for a long time and do not see the answer. We may think God hasn't heard or doesn't care. However, we are not to faint. I once witnessed the joy of one who had just received word that her brother had become a Christian. With tears running down her cheeks, she said, as she related her inspiring experience, "I have prayed for him for forty years." Rubinstein, the famous composer and pianist, once said, "If I fail to practice one day, I notice it; if two days, my friends notice it; if three days, my public notices it."

~ Millie Stamm

RELATIONSHIPS

A friend loves at all times,
and a brother is born for adversity.

PROVERBS 17:17

My intercessor is my friend
as my eyes pour out tears to God.

JOB 16:20

He who covers over an offense promotes love,
but whoever repeats the matter separates close
friends.

PROVERBS 17:9

Love one another deeply, from the heart.

1 PETER 1:22

Wounds from a friend can be trusted,
but an enemy multiplies kisses.

PROVERBS 27:6

*Jesus said, "Greater love has no one than
this, that he lay down his life for his friends.
You are my friends if you do what I command."*

JOHN 15:13–14

The pleasantness of one's friend springs
from his earnest counsel.

PROVERBS 27:9

Two are better than one,
　　because they have a good return for their
　　work:
If one falls down,
　　his friend can help him up.
But pity the [one] who falls
　　and has no one to help him up!

ECCLESIASTES 4:9–10

*Carry each other's burdens, and in this way
you will fulfill the law of Christ.*

GALATIANS 6:2

*If we walk in the light, as he is in the light,
we have fellowship with one another.*

1 JOHN 1:7

*Just as each of us has one body with many
members, and these members do not all have
the same function, so in Christ we who are many form one
body, and each member belongs to all the others.*

ROMANS 12:4–5

*Be completely humble and gentle; be patient, bearing with
one another in love. Make every effort to keep the
unity of the Spirit through the bond of peace.*

EPHESIANS 4:2–3

*If anyone has material possessions and
sees his brother in need but has no pity on him,
how can the love of God be in him? Dear children,
let us not love with words or tongue
but with actions and in truth.*

1 JOHN 3:17–18

GOD'S
FRIENDS

*H*OW DO YOU LIKE YOUR FRIENDS? DO YOU LIKE THEM TO BE faithful and loyal? Encouraging, thoughtful, and kind? But how many of your friends would measure up to such standards?

Friends are people, and people are not always faithful and kind. Just look at some of the people Jesus called his friends. Peter was always interrupting and telling Jesus what he should do. Then there was Mary Magdalene, whose sordid past was well known. Mary, the sister of Martha, failed as a housekeeper. Indecisive Thomas never stood up for his opinions. Then there was Nicodemus, a chicken for not showing his face in the daytime.

These people had their problems. Nevertheless, Jesus valued them as friends. He didn't expect them to be perfect; he expected them to be themselves, faults and fine points together. And all he asked of them was their love. Love for him and for each other.

Perhaps you're the type who forgets appointments or birthdays. Maybe in a group, you talk too much or don't talk at all. Housecleaning doesn't top your priority list. You get intimidated easily and fail to stick up for your friends. Aren't you glad that none of these things disqualify you from your Lord's circle of friends?

Jesus says that you are his friend if you do two things: Love God and love others.

~Joni Eareckson Tada

GOD'S WORDS OF LIFE ON

REST

*Jesus said, "Come to me, all you who are weary
and burdened, and I will give you rest. Take my yoke
upon you and learn from me, for I am gentle
and humble in heart, and you will find rest for
your souls. For my yoke is easy and my burden is light."*

MATTHEW 11:28–30

The LORD gives strength to the weary
    and increases the power of the weak.
Even youths grow tired and weary,
    and young men stumble and fall;
but those who hope in the LORD
    will renew their strength.
They will soar on wings like eagles;
    they will run and not grow weary,
    they will walk and not be faint.

ISAIAH 40:29–31

*"I will refresh the weary and satisfy
the faint," says the LORD.*

JEREMIAH 31:25

The LORD makes me lie down in green pastures,
he leads me beside quiet waters,
    he restores my soul.
He guides me in paths of righteousness
    for his name's sake.

PSALM 23:2–3

The apostles gathered around Jesus and
reported to him all they had done and taught.
Then, because so many people were coming and
going that they did not even have a chance
to eat, he said to them, "Come with me by
yourselves to a quiet place and get some rest."

MARK 6:30–31

Find rest, O my soul, in God alone;
    my hope comes from him.

PSALM 62:5

Restore us, O God;
　　　make your face shine upon us.

PSALM 80:3

*The LORD said, "My Presence will
go with you, and I will give you rest."*

EXODUS 33:14

Let the beloved of the LORD rest secure in him,
　　　for he shields him all day long,
　　　and the one the LORD loves rests between
　　　his shoulders.

DEUTERONOMY 33:12

Be at rest once more, O my soul,
　　　for the LORD has been good to you.

PSALM 116:7

IN REST,
FIND GOD

*I*N THE SOLITUDE OF A CAVE ELIJAH EXPERIENCED GOD'S AWESOME healing and saving power. The Lord had allowed Elijah to rest for a moment before reminding him that he understood and knew his pain.

Elijah came out of the cave and found that the Lord was an ever-present reality. Elijah was not alone! The earthquake and the fire both got his attention. Yet, it was in the still, small voice—a whisper from God—that Elijah rediscovered the Lord for himself.

Perhaps out of Elijah's experience we can find hope and help for our own lives. God made a time and place for Elijah to pull away from his ministry to rest. In the same way, God allows us to retreat and rest from our weariness and fears. He gives us this time to allow ourselves to relax physically, spiritually, and mentally so that we can recognize the presence of God.

We often feel alone because God does not manifest himself in our lives with great fanfare but in quiet, barely perceptible ways. Perhaps we can learn to be still and sit silently so we can recognize the presence of God. As the psalmist said, "Be still, and know that I am God" (Psalm 46:10). For the Lord is always faithful to his Word, saying, "Never will I leave you; never will I forsake you" (Hebrews 13:5).

-Reverend Dr. Cheryl Clemetson

SELF-IMAGE

*Your beauty should not come from outward
adornment, such as braided hair and the
wearing of gold jewelry and fine clothes.
Instead, it should be that of your inner self,
the unfading beauty of a gentle and quiet
spirit, which is of great worth in God's sight.*

1 PETER 3:3–4

*Jesus said, "Are not two sparrows sold for a penny?
Yet not one of them will fall to the ground
apart from the will of your Father. And even
the very hairs of your head are all numbered.
So don't be afraid; you are worth more
than many sparrows."*

MATTHEW 10:29–31

*The Spirit himself testifies with our spirit that we are God's
children. Now if we are children, then we are heirs—
heirs of God and co-heirs with Christ, if indeed we
share in his sufferings in order that we
may also share in his glory.*

ROMANS 8:16–17

*How great is the love the Father has
lavished on us, that we should be
called children of God! And that is what we are!*

1 JOHN 3:1

*God chose us in him before the creation of the world to
be holy and blameless in his sight. In love he predestined
us to be adopted as his sons through Jesus Christ, in
accordance with his pleasure and will—to the praise
of his glorious grace, which he has freely
given us in the One he loves.*

EPHESIANS 1:4–6

*God has reconciled you by Christ's physical
body through death to present you holy
in his sight, without blemish and free from accusation.*

COLOSSIANS 1:22

*You have put on the new self, which is being renewed in
knowledge in the image of its Creator.*

COLOSSIANS 3:10

For you created my inmost being;
    you knit me together in my mother's womb.
I praise you because I am fearfully and wonderfully made;
    your works are wonderful,
    I know that full well.

PSALM 139:13–14

*God created man in his own image,
in the image of God he created him;
male and female he created them.*

GENESIS 1:27

*For we are God's workmanship, created in
Christ Jesus to do good works, which God
prepared in advance for us to do.*

EPHESIANS 2:10

Charm is deceptive, and beauty is fleeting;
    but a woman who fears the LORD is to
    be praised.

PROVERBS 31:30

ANOREXIC
FAITH

I WAS STRUGGLING WITH ANOREXIA NERVOSA. I HAD BEEN OBSESSED with everything about my physical appearance. God tells me that the condition of my heart is important to him, much more important than the condition of my body. I had placed my hope, not in God's unconditional love, but in controlling my weight.

When I sank below eighty pounds, my internal battle intensified. I was a Christian, desiring to serve God, yet enslaved to food. I was miserable. Night after night I sobbed into my pillow, pleading that God would make me normal.

He answered those prayers slowly and gently. First, he showed me my sin and forgave me. He gave me caring friends to talk to, reassurance from his Word, and a wonderful husband. Michael loves me, not my dress size!

And, as confirmation that my healing is complete, God has given us three beautiful children—our three miracles, we call them, since I was told I would never be able to bear children as a result of my anorexia.

Now I desire only to fear God and put my hope in his love ... and through his strength, I will delight only in him!

–Debbie Smith

SERVING

*Jesus said, "Whoever wants to save his life will
lose it, but whoever loses his life for me will find it."*

MATTHEW 16:25

*Jesus knew that the Father had put all things
under his power, and that he had come from
God and was returning to God; so he got up from the meal,
took off his outer clothing, and wrapped a towel around his
waist. After that, he poured water into a basin and began to
wash his disciples' feet, drying them with the towel that was
wrapped around him. ... When he had finished washing their
feet, he put on his clothes and returned to his place. "Do you
understand what I have done for you?" he asked them.
"You call me 'Teacher' and 'Lord,' and rightly so, for that
is what I am. Now that I, your Lord and Teacher,
have washed your feet, you also should wash one
another's feet. I have set you an example that you
should do as I have done for you.*

JOHN 13:3–5, 12–15

*Serve God faithfully with all your heart; consider
what great things he has done for you.*

1 SAMUEL 12:24

Jesus loves us and has freed us from our sins by his blood, and has made us to be a kingdom and priests to serve his God and Father—to him be glory and power for ever and ever!

REVELATION 1:5–6

Serve one another in love.

GALATIANS 5:13

Each one should use whatever gift he has received to serve others, faithfully administering God's grace in its various forms. If anyone speaks, he should do it as one speaking the very words of God. If anyone serves, he should do it with the strength God provides, so that in all things God may be praised through Jesus Christ.

1 PETER 4:10–11

Those who have served well gain an excellent standing and great assurance in their faith in Christ Jesus.

1 TIMOTHY 3:13

I thank Christ Jesus our Lord, who has given me strength, that he considered me faithful, appointing me to his service.

1 TIMOTHY 1:12

Be shepherds of God's flock that is under your care, serving as overseers—not because you must, but because you are willing, as God wants you to be. ... And when the Chief Shepherd appears, you will receive the crown of glory that will never fade away.

1 PETER 5:2, 4

It is the LORD your God you must follow, and him you must revere. Keep his commands and obey him; serve him and hold fast to him.

DEUTERONOMY 13:4

If serving the LORD seems undesirable to you, then choose for yourselves this day whom you will serve ... . But as for me and my household, we will serve the LORD.

JOSHUA 24:15

SERVING A
WORTHY MASTER

*B*EING A SERVANT IS ONE OF THE MOST IMPORTANT LESSONS FOR Christians to learn; but unfortunately, we often have to work through gross misconceptions. We have fears about entrusting ourselves to any boss, but we must learn in our spiritual journey that this Master is unlike any other. He will not abuse us or misuse us. He has our greatest interest at heart. He encourages us through our servanthood to be all that we can be and then gives us his own Holy Spirit to empower us to become so. This Master is one who even laid down his life for those who were his servants.

He is a Master unlike any other. Not to be feared, he is worthy of our service.

Many of us think servanthood means losing ourselves in such a way that we become people without personality, people without original thinking ability, people without giftedness. But when one serves this Master, the opposite is true: He makes us full, complete human beings filled with his own image, with his own amazing mentality. Paradoxically, while teaching us to be more like him, we become more of whom he created us to be.

~Karen Burton Mains

Whoever lives by the truth comes into the light, so that it may be seen plainly that what he has done has been done through God.

JOHN 3:21

Those who live according to the sinful nature have their minds set on what that nature desires; but those who live in accordance with the Spirit have their minds set on what the Spirit desires.

ROMANS 8:5

What does the LORD require of you?
To act justly and to love mercy
and to walk humbly with your God.

MICAH 6:8

Jesus said, "If anyone loves me, he will obey my teaching. My Father will love him, and we will come to him and make our home with him."

JOHN 14:23

The grace of God that brings salvation has appeared to all men. It teaches us to say "No" to ungodliness and worldly passions, and to live self-controlled, upright and godly lives in this present age.

TITUS 2:11–12

Forgetting what is behind and straining toward what is ahead, I press on toward the goal to win the prize for which God has called me heavenward in Christ Jesus.

PHILIPPIANS 3:13–14

Jesus said: "Whoever believes in me, as the Scripture has said, streams of living water will flow from within him."

JOHN 7:38

Grow in the grace and knowledge of our Lord and Savior Jesus Christ. To him be glory both now and forever!

2 PETER 3:18

Make every effort to add to your faith goodness; and to goodness, knowledge; and to knowledge, self-control; and to self-control, perseverance; and to perseverance, godliness; and to godliness, brotherly kindness; and to brotherly kindness, love. For if you possess these qualities in increasing measure, they will keep you from being ineffective and unproductive in your knowledge of our Lord Jesus Christ.

2 PETER 1:5–8

Jesus said, "I tell you the truth, no one can enter the kingdom of God unless he is born of water and the Spirit. Flesh gives birth to flesh, but the Spirit gives birth to spirit. You should not be surprised at my saying, 'You must be born again.' The wind blows wherever it pleases. You hear its sound, but you cannot tell where it comes from or where it is going. So it is with everyone born of the Spirit."

JOHN 3:5–8

I tell you that no one who is speaking by the Spirit of God says, "Jesus be cursed," and no one can say, "Jesus is Lord," except by the Holy Spirit.

1 CORINTHIANS 12:3

THE RIVER OF
THE HOLY SPIRIT

JESUS SAID, "WHOEVER BELIEVES IN ME ... STREAMS OF LIVING water will flow from within him" (John 7:38). This refers not to water but to the Holy Spirit who, when turned loose in our lives, strengthens, grows, and gives us vibrancy. As we allow the Holy Spirit to proceed from God and grow stronger, deeper, wider, and more pervasive, our spiritual and physical person takes on new, eternal, and abundant life. Only as we allow the Holy Spirit to flow in our thoughts, emotions, will, desires, dispositions, actions and activities does spiritual transformation take place. Then people can look at us in the midst of tribulation and say, "I think I see the Son of God." Our captors can look in the fiery furnaces and see us walk in confidence as we are accompanied by the fourth man.

I want God's waters to flow deeply and widely and expansively throughout this being of mine. I want the river of the Holy Spirit to so fill and guide me that I become a remote temple from which a branch of God's river can flow. I pray that God will let the waters flow in me, as I pray you will ask God to let his waters flow in you.

–Reverend Dr. Alicia D. Byrd

TALENTS

*There are different kinds of gifts, but the same Spirit.
There are different kinds of service, but the
same Lord. There are different kinds of working,
but the same God works all of them in all men.*

*Now to each one the manifestation of the Spirit is given for the
common good. To one there is given through the Spirit the message of wisdom, to another the message of knowledge by means
of the same Spirit, to another faith by the same Spirit, to
another gifts of healing by that one Spirit, to another miracu-
lous powers, to another prophecy, to another distinguishing
between spirits, to another speaking in different kinds of
tongues, and to still another the interpretation of tongues. All
these are the work of one and the same Spirit, and he gives
them to each one, just as he determines.*

1 CORINTHIANS 12:4–11

*You do not lack any spiritual gift as you eagerly
wait for our Lord Jesus Christ to be revealed.*

1 CORINTHIANS 1:7

Every good and perfect gift is from above,
coming down from the Father of the heavenly
lights, who does not change like shifting shadows.

JAMES 1:17

I remind you to fan into flame
the gift of God, which is in you.

2 TIMOTHY 1:6

Each one should use whatever gift he has received to
serve others, faithfully administering God's grace in its
various forms. If anyone speaks, he should do it as one
speaking the very words of God. If anyone serves, he should
do it with the strength God provides, so that in all things
God may be praised through Jesus Christ. To him be
the glory and the power for ever and ever. Amen.

1 PETER 4:10–11

Since you are eager to have spiritual gifts,
try to excel in gifts that build up the church.

1 CORINTHIANS 14:12

We have different gifts, according to the grace given us. If a man's gift is prophesying, let him use it in proportion to his faith. If it is serving, let him serve; if it is teaching, let him teach; if it is encouraging, let him encourage; if it is contributing to the needs of others, let him give generously; if it is leadership, let him govern diligently; if it is showing mercy, let him do it cheerfully.

ROMANS 12:6–8

Remember the LORD your God, for it is he who gives you the ability to produce wealth.

DEUTERONOMY 8:18

Now it is required that those who have been given a trust must prove faithful.

1 CORINTHIANS 4:2

"[The master of the servant in Jesus' parable] replied, 'Well done, good and faithful servant! You have been faithful with a few things; I will put you in charge of many things. Come and share your master's happiness!'"

MATTHEW 25:21

GOD'S TOOLS

*T*HERE IS A STORY TOLD ABOUT A HOUSE THAT WAS BADLY IN need of paint. "I am going to paint the house," said a can of paint, waiting, already mixed, in a shed. "No, I am going to paint it," the brush asserted, bristling with impatience. "You are, are you?" sneered the ladder, lying against the wall. "How far would either of you go without me?" "Or without me to pay the bill?" arrogantly added the checkbook belonging to the owner of the house, in a voice muffled by the pocket of the coat hanging on a nail. Just then the painter, who had overheard the proud remarks, ventured to put in a word. "Perhaps I'd better take a holiday," he said quietly. "I wonder if the house would be painted by the time I got back."

Even the most efficient among us are only tools in the hands of the Great Master Worker. As we work with him and for him, he works in us and through us. One worker is not more valuable or important than another. He that plants and he that waters have a unity of purpose. There is no reason for rivalry. Each has his task; each has his place. Perhaps it is our task to plant—or it may be to water. There may be times when we plant and other times when we water. But whatever our place may be, we are laboring with and for God. Then God will give the increase.

—Millie Stamm

TRUST

Those who know your name will trust in you,
> for you, LORD, have never forsaken those who
> seek you.

PSALM 9:10

Those who trust in the LORD are like Mount Zion,
> which cannot be shaken but endures forever.

PSALM 125:1

Trust in the LORD forever,
> for the LORD, the LORD, is the Rock eternal.

ISAIAH 26:4

The LORD longs to be gracious to you;
> he rises to show you compassion.
For the LORD is a God of justice.
> Blessed are all who wait for him!

ISAIAH 30:18

Trust in the LORD and do good;
    dwell in the land and enjoy safe pasture.

PSALM 37:3

Whoever gives heed to instruction prospers,
    and blessed is he who trusts in the LORD.

PROVERBS 16:20

Blessed is the man who trusts in the LORD,
    whose confidence is in him.
He will be like a tree planted by the water
    that sends out its roots by the stream.
It does not fear when heat comes;
    its leaves are always green.
It has no worries in a year of drought
    and never fails to bear fruit.

JEREMIAH 17:7–8

Nebuchadnezzar said, "Praise be to the God of Shadrach, Meshach and Abednego, who has sent his angel and rescued his servants! They trusted in him and defied the king's command and were willing to give up their lives rather than serve or worship any god except their own God."

DANIEL 3:28

He who trusts in the Lord will prosper.

PROVERBS 28:25

Anyone who trusts in God will never be put to shame.

ROMANS 10:11

Whoever trusts in the Lord is kept safe.

PROVERBS 29:25

FREEDOM TO TRUST

*T*RUST IS SUCH A LOVELY WORD IN A WORLD THOROUGHLY SELF-indulged and complicated. It is quiet. Simple. It represents freedom. Rest. Letting go.

A friend of ours, who had been down the battered road of infertility, longed for another baby. A perfect situation came about— a young birth mother who felt the only answer for her baby was adoption.

A precious baby girl was born. The adoptive couple came from another city to meet the birth mother and to take their new baby home. The birth mother signed the papers, releasing the baby from the hospital. But in the courtroom, days later, she broke down. She just couldn't give up her baby.

The couple's celebration turned to heartbreak. Immediately, they began to trust; not to figure it all out, or judge the birth mother. They waited quietly. In a year, twin girls were born and theirs was the chosen family. They lost one, and God gave them back two.

There are very many unknowns in life. A husband's job. Our children's struggles. A tentative move. Critical talk behind our backs. A search for our own identity. Bills to pay. Aged parents to look after.

Let go completely. Trust. Live with it all in an open hand before God. Jesus promises he WILL work it all out.

~ Ann Kiemel Anderson

WISDOM

I guide you in the way of wisdom
    and lead you along straight paths.
When you walk, your steps will not be hampered;
    when you run, you will not stumble.

PROVERBS 4:11–12

Get wisdom, get understanding;
    do not forget my words or swerve from them.
Do not forsake wisdom, and she will protect you;
    love her, and she will watch over you.
Wisdom is supreme; therefore get wisdom.
    Though it cost all you have, get understanding.

PROVERBS 4:5–7

Know also that wisdom is sweet to your soul;
    if you find it, there is a future hope for you,
    and your hope will not be cut off.

PROVERBS 24:14

"I will instruct you and teach you in the way you
        should go;
    I will counsel you and watch over you,"
    says the LORD.

PSALM 32:8

*The wisdom that comes from heaven is first of
all pure; then peace-loving, considerate, submissive,
full of mercy and good fruit, impartial and sincere.*

JAMES 3:17

*If any of you lacks wisdom, he should ask
God, who gives generously to all without
finding fault, and it will be given to him.*

JAMES 1:5

*For the foolishness of God is wiser than
man's wisdom, and the weakness of God
is stronger than man's strength.*

1 CORINTHIANS 1:25

If you accept my words
     and store up my commands within you,
turning your ear to wisdom
     and applying your heart to understanding,
and if you call out for insight
     and cry aloud for understanding,
and if you look for it as for silver
     and search for it as for hidden treasure,
then you will understand the fear of the LORD
     and find the knowledge of God.
For the LORD gives wisdom,
     and from his mouth come knowledge and
     understanding.

PROVERBS 2:1–6

The fear of the Lord is the beginning of wisdom;
     all who follow his precepts have good
     understanding.

PSALM 111:10

INCREASING
IN WISDOM

*W*ISDOM COMES WHEN WE EXAMINE THE EXPERIENCES GOD gives us and discern what we have (or should have) learned from them. Nothing that has happened to us should be wasted (Romans 8:28). Because it is sometimes painful, often we do not take the time or effort to discover the reason for the "gift" of our personal experiences. When we do not learn as we should, we stop growing until we learn those same lessons through another experience tailor-made by God to make us mature (James 1:2–4). Most often we gain insight into our experiences only after earnest, persistent prayer. Psalm 43 is a
wonderful model of persistent prayer; it opens up to us a person searching to know what God wants to reveal about a specific experience.

Perhaps we should try writing out what we have learned about God, ourselves and life during and then after an important experience. As we learn these lessons, I think we'll find that we will not need to learn them again in exactly the same way! This increases our individual capacity to learn greater lessons and gain deeper wisdom (Matthew 13:12).

–Rosemary Jensen

WORRY

Cast your cares on the LORD
    and he will sustain you;
    he will never let the righteous fall.

PSALM 55:22

Commit your way to the LORD;
    trust in him and he will do this:
He will make your righteousness shine like the dawn,
    the justice of your cause like the noonday sun.

PSALM 37:5–6

*Do not worry about tomorrow, for tomorrow will
worry about itself. Each day has enough trouble of its own.*

MATTHEW 6:34

*Do not be anxious about anything, but
in everything, by prayer and petition, with thanksgiving,
present your requests to God. And the peace of God,
which transcends all understanding, will guard
your hearts and your minds in Christ Jesus.*

PHILIPPIANS 4:6–7

Keep your lives free from the love of money and be content with what you have, because God has said, "Never will I leave you; never will I forsake you."

HEBREWS 13:5

Cast all your anxiety on him because he cares for you.

1 PETER 5:7

Jesus said to his disciples: "I tell you, do not worry about your life, what you will eat; or about your body, what you will wear. Life is more than food, and the body more than clothes. Consider the ravens: They do not sow or reap, they have no storeroom or barn; yet God feeds them. And how much more valuable you are than birds! Who of you by worrying can add a single hour to his life?"

LUKE 12:22–25

Those who trust in the LORD are like Mount Zion, which cannot be shaken but endures forever.

PSALM 125:1

The LORD himself goes before you and will be with you;
he will never leave you nor forsake you. Do not
be afraid; do not be discouraged.

DEUTERONOMY 31:8

We say with confidence,
"The Lord is my helper; I will not be afraid.
What can man do to me?"

HEBREWS 13:6

Blessed is the man who trusts in the LORD,
whose confidence is in him.
He will be like a tree planted by the water
that sends out its roots by the stream.
It does not fear when heat comes;
its leaves are always green.
It has no worries in a year of drought
and never fails to bear fruit.

JEREMIAH 17:7–8

TAKING AND LEAVING
YOUR BURDENS

I KNEW A CHRISTIAN LADY WHO HAD A VERY HEAVY TEMPORAL burden ... One day, when it seemed especially heavy, she noticed lying on the table near her a little tract. She picked it up and began to read it, little knowing, however, that it was to create a revolution in her whole experience.

The story was of a poor woman who had been carried triumphantly through a life of unusual sorrow. She was giving the history of her life to a kind visitor on one occasion, and at the close the visitor said feelingly, "I do not see how you could bear so much sorrow!"

"I did not bear it," was the quick reply; "the Lord bore it for me."

"Yes," said the visitor, "that is the right way. We must take our troubles to the Lord." [The poor woman replied,] "We must do more than that: we must leave them there. Most people take their burdens to him, but they bring them away with them again, and are just as worried and unhappy as ever. But I take mine and I leave them with him, and come away and forget them. If the worry comes back, I take it to him again; and I do this over and over, until at last I just forget I have any worries."

-Hannah Whitall Smith

ACKNOWLEDGMENTS

Excerpts taken from:

The African-American Devotional Bible: New International Version. Copyright © 1997 by The Zondervan Corporation. All rights reserved. Devotional thoughts by Reverend Dr. Cheryl Clemetson, Reverend Rosalyn Grant Frederick, Reverend Dr. Delores Carpenter, and Reverend Dr. Alicia D. Byrd taken respectively from pp. 366, 634, 692, and 908.

Diamonds in the Dust by Joni Eareckson Tada. Copyright ©1993 by Joni Eareckson Tada. (Grand Rapids, MI: Zondervan Publishing House, 1993). All rights reserved. Devotional thoughts taken from March 27, June 26, September 4, October 2 & 23, and November 17.

Meditation Moments by Millie Stamm. Formerly published as *Meditation Moments for Women.* Copyright © 1967 by Zondervan Publishing House. (Grand Rapids, MI: Zondervan Publishing House, 1967)All rights reserved. Devotional thoughts taken from January 13, February 28, and March 21.

A Rose by any Other Name Would Still Have Aphids by Mab Graff Hoover. Copyright © 1992 by Mab Graff Hoover. All rights reserved. Devotional thoughts taken from pp. 40-41, 106-108.

At Inspirio we love to hear from you—
your stories, your feedback,
and your product ideas.
Please send your comments
to us by way of e-mail at
icares@zondervan.com
or to the address below:

inspirio

Attn: Inspirio Cares
5300 Patterson Avenue SE
Grand Rapids, MI 49530

If you would like further information
about Inspirio and the products
we create please visit us at:
www.inspiriogifts.com

Thank you and God Bless!